EXPLORING
with James Cook

CAPTAIN JAMES COOK, F.R.S.

by Cynthia Clampitt

PEARSON

Scott
Foresman

Editorial Offices: Glenview, Illinois • Parsippany, New Jersey • New York, New York

Sales Offices: Needham, Massachusetts • Duluth, Georgia • Glenview, Illinois
Coppell, Texas • Sacramento, California • Mesa, Arizona

James Cook was born in a cottage in northern England similar to this one.

James Cook's Childhood

James Cook's father was a poor farmworker from Scotland. He had moved to northern England to find work. His son James was born in a small farming village on October 27, 1728.

A farmer who had hired James's father noticed how smart James was. The farmer offered to send James to school. From the age of eight to the age of twelve, James studied reading, writing, and arithmetic. He still had to help his father on the farm, but he spent his free time studying. He loved learning—and learning would be something he did for the rest of his life.

When James Cook was sixteen, he got a job at a store in a nearby village. The village was close to Whitby, a busy port filled with ships. Cook watched the ships come in and out of the port. He talked to the sailors. He studied anything he thought might help him if he ever had the chance to go to sea.

Cook did a good job at the store, but the shopkeeper could see that Cook was more interested in the ships. After a year and a half, the shopkeeper introduced Cook to a ship owner in Whitby. Cook's life at sea had begun.

In the English town of Whitby, Cook first came in contact with ships and the sea.

Cook's First Years at Sea

Cook spent the next eight years learning about ships and sailing. The Whitby ships sailed the dangerous waters of the North Sea. Learning to sail here prepared Cook to sail anywhere.

Cook's skills and knowledge grew. He was offered a promotion in Whitby, but he thought that Britain's navy would give him more chances to see the world.

Life in the navy was not easy. Ships were crowded and trips were long. Many men died of **scurvy**, a disease caused by a lack of vitamin C. Cook obeyed orders and worked hard. Soon he had command of his own ship.

The Seven Years' War

The Seven Years' War lasted from 1756 to 1763. All of the major European powers of that time took part in it. While much of the war happened in Europe, some of it was fought in North America. The North American part of the war actually began in 1754. This war is known in the United States as the French and Indian War.

James Cook learned to make accurate maps, such as this one of Newfoundland.

The Seven Years' War began in 1756. In 1757 Cook was sent to Canada. There he met a man who taught him the science of surveying. Surveying is the careful measuring of the size, shape, and location of places.

Surveying was a new science, but Cook knew that it would become an important one. He studied hard and was soon a skilled surveyor. Cook's survey of the St. Lawrence River helped Britain win an important battle in Quebec, Canada. Cook began surveying full-time. From 1763 to 1768, he surveyed eastern Canada and created detailed maps.

Let the Exploration Begin

Cook was an excellent surveyor and mapmaker. He was also a scientist, a mathematician, an artist, and a writer. A report that he wrote about the Sun and Moon made people realize he could do more than sail a ship. His life was about to change. He was about to become an explorer too.

Many people in Britain thought that exploring the unknown parts of the world was important. James Cook was perfect for this work. Cook was asked to make a long **voyage**, or journey by sea, to the far side of the world.

This British map shows the routes of Cook's three voyages of exploration.

In Tahiti people who lived there paddled their canoes out to greet Cook's ship.

In August 1768 James Cook set sail on the *Endeavour*. Cook made sure his ship was clean and his crew had a healthy diet. He believed that if his men ate the right food, they would not die of scurvy.

First Cook would sail to Tahiti to observe the planet Venus passing in front of the Sun. Measuring this would make it possible to mathematically figure out the distance between Earth and the Sun. Then Cook and his crew were to explore the southern **latitudes**, to see if there was another continent south of the **equator**.

After his project in Tahiti was finished, Cook found New Zealand. He charted New Zealand's entire coast. Six months later, he came to the east coast of Australia. Cook charted this 2,000-mile-long coast as well. Many discoveries were made. The botanists, or plant scientists, on the voyage found so many new plants in one place that Cook named the spot Botany Bay.

Finally, in 1771, the *Endeavour* headed back toward England. All of Cook's achievements were important, but one was a real surprise: In three years at sea, Cook had not lost anyone to scurvy. This had never happened before. Cook's ideas about health and diet had been right.

This stamp from 1940 shows Cook, his ship, and Cook's chart of New Zealand.

This picture was created by an artist on Cook's second voyage. Cook's ship is seen among icebergs near Antarctica.

Cook's Second Voyage

In the 1700s many people in the **Northern Hemisphere** believed that there must be another continent in the **Southern Hemisphere**. Cook was asked to go on another voyage.

Cook departed in July 1772. He took with him the first clock that would work on a ship. This clock made it possible for Cook to figure out **longitude**. Longitude had never been accurately measured before. Figuring out longitude helped Cook identify the location of many places.

On this voyage, Cook commanded the *Resolution*. He sailed south from England, into the **frigid** waters around Antarctica. Cook and his crews were the first people to travel south of the Antarctic Circle.

Cook felt certain that there was land under the ice. He also believed that this was the last continent that would be discovered in the Southern Hemisphere. He was right.

As Cook sailed closer to Antarctica, the terrible cold froze the ships' ropes and sails. Surrounded by broken ice and towering icebergs, the ships were in danger of being crushed. Cook's ships and his crews sailed to within one hundred miles of the coast of Antarctica, but were forced to give up.

Cook headed into the South Pacific, where he found and mapped many unfamiliar islands. After a few more months, he turned back toward Antarctica. He sailed all the rest of the way around the frozen continent before heading back to England.

Cook reached home in July 1775. This second voyage had taken more than three years and had covered seventy thousand miles.

CAPTAIN JAMES COOK, F.R.S.

PAINTED BY W.W. HODGES   ENGRAVED BY J. BASIRE

James Cook wrote about all the places he traveled.

James Cook spent most of his adult life sailing the world's oceans.

Cook's Final Voyage

In the 1700s people still wondered whether there was an ocean passage above North America connecting the Atlantic and Pacific Oceans. Cook was now forty-seven years old. He had spent nearly thirty years at sea. He was tired and his health was not good. Could he be asked to lead another expedition?

Cook understood how important the discovery of a Northwest Passage would be to Britain. He agreed to command this voyage and departed in July 1776.

Captain Cook again sailed on the *Resolution*. There was also a second ship, the *Discovery*. The two ships sailed below Africa and into the Pacific Ocean. Traveling north, Cook found many new islands, including the Hawaiian Islands. The ships stopped in Hawaii for supplies. The island people seemed friendly and happy to trade for food.

From Hawaii, Cook sailed to North America. He explored the coast of what is now Oregon, Washington, and Alaska. Traveling up the coast, Cook and his crew met many new people.

Views like this would have greeted Cook and his crew as they sailed along the coast of Alaska.

Captain Cook sailed to the Hawaiian Islands on his third voyage.

Cook sailed through the Aleutian Islands, the string of islands in Alaska's far west. From here, he sailed into the Arctic Ocean. Ahead of him were massive walls of ice. Cook got as close to the ice walls as he could. But there was no passage through to the Atlantic, only great danger from the moving ice. Disappointed, Cook turned west, where he charted part of the coast of Siberia.

Winter was coming. Cook felt that warm weather would be healthy for his crew. It was a difficult decision, but Cook and his men returned to Hawaii.

In January of the next year, Cook again sailed north. He still wanted to try to find a way through the Arctic Ocean.

When one of the ships was damaged in a storm, he was forced to return to Hawaii. This time the Hawaiians were not happy to see Cook and his men. On February 14, 1779, several Hawaiian warriors met Cook on the beach and killed him. Cook's saddened crew sailed back to England with the news.

James Cook is still honored today in many countries. Some people consider him to be the world's greatest explorer.

This statue of James Cook stands in London, England.

Glossary

equator the imaginary line that circles the center of Earth from east to west

frigid very cold

latitude the measurement of how far north or south of the equator a place is located

longitude the measurement of how far east or west of the prime meridian a place is located

Northern Hemisphere the half of Earth north of the equator

scurvy a disease caused by a lack of vitamin C

Southern Hemisphere the half of Earth south of the equator

voyage a journey by sea